"Ravi takes a scholarly yet imaginative approach to apologetics. The dialogue he sets forth in this unique drama will educate, enthrall, and enlighten you—and everyone you share it with—for years to come."

BRUCE WILKINSON, AUTHOR OF THE
#1 *NEW YORK TIMES* BESTSELLER *THE PRAYER OF JABEZ*

"The works of Ravi Zacharias are a vital resource around our house, and this latest addition to our intellectual arsenal is delightfully different: a vivid, dramatized meeting of the minds through which the truth of the gospel—and Dr. Zacharias's impeccable logic—shines forth with enjoyable clarity."

FRANK PERETTI

"Ravi Zacharias is a first-rate thinker and a preeminent Christian apologist. With *The Lotus and the Cross,* Zacharias now demonstrates that he is also a gifted and imaginative writer. This captivating dialogue not only clears up confusion about the claims of Christ and Buddha, but also provides us with a highly entertaining read."

CHUCK COLSON

"With signs of spiritual warfare all around us, this book challenges all Christians—male and female—to arm up and engage the enemy. Its pages are chock-full of fascinating insights and solid, practical, biblical advice. It's a must-read for everyone who takes seriously Christ's command to 'Fight the good fight.'"

MARY KASSIAN, PRESIDENT OF ALABASTER FLASK MINISTRIES

The Lotus and the Cross

Jesus Talks with Buddha

Ravi Zacharias

Multnomah Books

The Lotus and the Cross
Published by Multnomah Books
12265 Oracle Boulevard, Suite 200
Colorado Springs, Colorado 80921.

ISBN: 978-1-60142-318-4

Published in association with the literary agency of Wolgemuth & Associates Inc.

Published in the United States by WaterBrook Multnomah, an imprint of the Crown Publishing Group, a division of Random House Inc., New York.

The Library of Congress cataloged the hardcover edition as follows:

Zacharias, Ravi K.
New birth or rebirth? : Jesus talks with Krishna / Ravi K. Zacharias. — 1st ed.
p. cm.
1. Jesus Christ—Fiction. 2. Krishna (Hindu deity)—Fiction. 3. Imaginary conversations. I. Title.
PS3576.A19N49 2008
813'.54—dc22

2007047027

Printed in the United States of America
2010—First Trade Paperback Edition

10 9 8 7 6 5 4 3 2 1

To the kind and generous peoples of
Malaysia, India, Singapore, and Thailand
for their friendship, hospitality, and inspiration.

Acknowledgments

My heartfelt thanks goes out to many who have ably and sacrificially helped me bring this book together.

To Don Jacobson, for the idea of a conversational-style narrative that would plumb the differences between these two systems of belief but retain respect for both.

To Rod Morris, for his sensitive and capable final edits.

To all the Multnomah staff, for their encouragement and affirmation.

To the readers who freely offered their honest suggestions.

To Margie, my wife, who is my favorite critic and editor.

To the monks and nuns, for their energetic dialogues and openness in dealing with tough issues. I will forever be grateful to them.

To the wonderful people in Malaysia, Thailand, India, and Singapore that went out of their way to host my research and make my stays memorable.

This has been a rewarding journey of thought and imagination—and for that I am grateful most of all to God.

Introduction

Writing this book has been an incredible experience. I spent scores of hours in temples with monks and with instructors of students of Buddhist thought. The discussions I had were always cordial and delightful. Over many a cup of tea, we lingered and talked about life's deepest questions and contrasting answers.

Having enjoyed such rapport with those who embrace the Buddhist worldview, I found it difficult to highlight the deep differences between Buddhism and Christianity and not bring offense. Those differences may be discomforting, but they are real. Even the answers the monks gave to my questions were not always the same depending on which school of Buddhism they represented. At times there was frustration on their faces when the questions became tough and their answers dissimilar. But even in the midst of disagreements, they drew comfort from the fact that, for them, agreement was not as important as the pursuit itself.

I will always be grateful for their courtesy and hospitality. Although we have radically different answers to life's fundamental questions, we dare not shrink from asking the hard questions just to avoid discomfort.

Although a book like this could be slanted any way one pleases, some fundamental ideas are inescapable and must be engaged. In that sense, at least, I trust I have presented the ideas fairly and subjected them to scrutiny. Many of those I talked with will be reading this, and I look forward to their responses.

Jesus and Buddha cannot both be right. The lotus is the symbol of Buddhism; the cross, the symbol of the Christian faith. Behind the two symbols stand two diametrically opposed beliefs. I ask you, the reader, to examine the message of each, using both your heart and your mind. It is worth the exercise because it will determine your destiny. One day we will all find out that being respectful and sincere does not give us license to be wrong. Truth demands investigation and commitment. Our conclusions must be in keeping with Truth that can be tested. To be handcuffed by a lie is the worst of all imprisonments.

May the God of all truth lead you to the Truth that sets you free indeed.

Prologue

It is the first blush of dawn as I step into this long-tailed boat after haggling with the boatman for a suitable price. His jolly countenance and leathery skin tell a story all their own. His toothless grin is a cartoonist's dream, and a comb has not visited his sparse scalp for ages. If one has to wake up this early, the sight of him beats the face of a clock any day.

He has agreed to take me on a journey along the famed River of Kings. We wend our way through back canals that teem with life, dotted by the corrugated iron rooftops along shores that house a large part of this megacity. A sense of nostalgia surfaces within me as the slumbering multitude begins to stir among the backdrop of temples and pagodas spiraling toward the sky. It is as if the calendar collides here, the past, present, and future all speaking in unison. The morning air is fragrant with aromas ranging from lemongrass to fish sauce, all being prepared for the day's consumption. Yes, the food here wins the palate of virtually every traveler. This is a city I have visited often and its people are among the most winsome in the world. The smiles, the graces, and the charms exude as in no other land I know. A carefree attitude toward life is writ large in the cultural ethos, and strangers make you feel very welcome, even when one may have just cheated you into buying a fake name-brand watch or a pirated copy of the latest movie.

I am very much at home on this continent, for it reminds me so much of the land of my birth. But there is a reality here that compels me to ask some hard questions about life. Within this culture, the most reverent of expressions mix with the most unashamed abandon for the sensual. I see a monk walking in the distance, a bowl for begging in his hand, but I also see a man who spends most of his day waylaying tourists and seducing them with pictures to come and visit a nearby brothel. He does that from dawn to dusk, seven days a week. It is quite a juxtaposition: the monk, austere and in pursuit of nirvana; the man, with a roguish smile, promising a different kind of bliss.

Here a cultural immersion would be impossible without visiting a host of temples—the Emerald Buddha, the Reclining Buddha, the Golden Buddha, and a long list of others. But here, too, the newspapers sound a somber tone. The income from prostitution, they declare, exceeds the entire national budget. Here, drugs and AIDS have ravaged the population, and sincere politicians are trying desperately to deal with it. But this very city is exploited by money-hungry opportunists who bring in planeloads of men, promising them orgies to fulfill every imaginable craving.

And so as I sit in this sputtering boat, smothered in a misty spray, I feel nearly drowned in a sea of emotions. How does one talk about the eternal when both religion and riotous living argue that nothing is permanent? An odd mix of the glory and the shame of humanity within this microcosm ignites a series of difficult questions.

As we make our way down the canal, able to look almost directly into the living quarters of those who live along its shores, I cannot shake the memory of a newspaper article on the front page the previous day. It told the story of a young, attractive woman who left home to earn a living, only to pay the heaviest price of all: the devastation of AIDS. This a summary of that story:

At seventeen, young and beautiful Priya decided to head to the big city to work. Within hours of her arrival, the very friend who had enticed her with the promise of big money mercilessly raped her. Thus began a fourteen-year stretch of untold heartache and tragedy. As if to mend Priya's torn spirit, the "friend" found her a job as a seamstress. But even there Priya found no relief from the plundering ways of those she had cast her lot with. She was soon being used and abused to deviant ends, only with a new twist—she was paid for satisfying their perverse pleasures. By the age of twenty-three she had become a full-fledged prostitute, managed by a handful of thugs who shared in the spoils.

Fate struck hard one day when she became pregnant. For a few months her profession was put on hold. Inevitably, financial strain set in, and she could hardly wait to give birth to the child so she could give it away, then return to the sordid life that had enslaved her.

But a more devastating shock awaited her: She discovered that she was HIV-positive. She could not discontinue her lifestyle, for she needed the money to treat her disease and hang onto life. Hardened, calloused, and almost vengeful, she continued to sell her services to hundreds of customers, including bankers, businessmen, and doctors, of whom she kept a detailed record. She knew she was signing each man's death warrant, but she was drowning in despair, and her life had lost all value.

Eventually she could no longer hide the disfiguring marks of her disease. Blisters blanketed her body. She resorted to desperate methods in search of a cure, even boiling a toad and drinking the water, a practice that villagers believed might cure her. She made numerous attempts to kill herself, only to fail each time. Finally Priya poisoned herself once more, and this time she set her house on fire and lay down for the last time, enshrouded in flames.

Her once-beautiful body was reduced to ashes. No one would even come close to her charred remains for fear of infection. She died alone. And not far from her others played the same deadly game, thinking that this same end would never be theirs.

How can I forget this story? My heart is heavy as I remember it. Are some of the faces I see this morning headed toward the same fearsome future? I am told that hundreds, if not thousands, have made their way to this very city over the years, and that the script has been the same for scores of them.

What, Lord Jesus, would You have said to Priya, had she brought her decrepit body and aching heart to You? (Actually, many women in similar situations did come to Jesus.)

And what would Buddha have said to her, this being a land where 95 percent of its people are Buddhists? Interestingly, the faces of suffering were what led Gautama (the birth name of Buddha) to pursue the answers to such grief, and in that pursuit, he became the Buddha, the "Enlightened One."

A waterfall of questions flows over me, and my mind is caught in a vortex of possibilities. What, I wonder, would Buddha or Jesus say to *each other* if they were in this boat with me, breathing the pungent smells, witnessing the extreme sights, hearing the lively sounds, and discussing the plight of this young woman? Many Buddhist scholars have drawn parallels between Buddha's and Jesus' teachings; one noted scholar even called them "brothers." Is that an accurate portrayal? Or did this scholar, among others, completely miss the fundamental differences?

I let my imagination take a ride and picture just such a conversation.

The Lotus and the Cross

Jesus Talks with Buddha

Jesus: Sit here next to me, Priya. And what a lovely name you have—*Priya,* meaning "sweetheart" or "beloved." Yet the stillness of the morning does not silence the scream of your heart, does it?

Priya: I can't resist a smile as I think of my name, even the way you pronounced it, Sir. Strange that you bring it up, though. To those who've known the unlovely side of my life, I've never used my real name. Sometimes I wonder if I knew anybody's real name there. All I know is that if my brothers and sisters saw me now...I don't know what they would call me.

Jesus: Have you seen your parents lately?

Priya: No. They send me messages. They expect to hear any day now that I have died.

Jesus: I've been thinking of them as I see you struggle in pain here. Names, at least in the minds of parents, are the embodiment of a hope with a destiny in mind. I'm sure this end is not what they envisioned...a heart full of grief, alone and torn apart, wishing only to die.

Priya: When each heartbeat sends a fresh, searing jolt of pain, why would I want it to keep beating? You know, we have a common saying in my culture when anything goes wrong—it basically means "Never mind" or "It will all work out." I heard it a dozen times a day growing up. But I don't believe that anymore. Life has not "worked out." Every tick of the clock makes me long for the day when I stop hearing it.

Yes, death would be welcome. As a matter of fact, I have tried, but…

Jesus: Your very face tells your story, Priya. Your whole body is like a gaping wound of the past.

You've hinted at a timeless truth, though, that time isn't just a fleeting thing. It never moves forward without engraving its mark upon the heart—sometimes a stab, sometimes a tender touch, sometimes a vise grip of spikes, sometimes a mortal wound. But always an imprint.

Priya: You don't think of that when you're young and carefree. But it doesn't take long to feel those imprints deep inside you.

Jesus: Which means, Priya, that these few moments we have together are not a meaningless exchange as you near the end of your life, but rather a real possibility as to how your story may end.

Here, have a drink of water. Your mouth is dry, and a ride in a boat on this torrid day will only intensify your thirst.

Priya: My drinking cup is in my bag. Let me get it…you shouldn't touch it. Oh, thank you, Sir! You're very kind.

Jesus: It didn't take long, did it, to find out that even those you trusted used you and abused you till you were nothing more than a body to them. How typical it is that the scavengers are never around after the flesh is consumed.

Time isn't just a
fleeting thing.
It never moves forward
without engraving its
mark upon the heart.

Priya: Sometimes I'm filled with anger toward them, Jesus, but frankly, sometimes I'm just too tired to be angry anymore...too tired to live.

Jesus: I understand. But it's not just the others, Priya. They become the natural target, but you found out some things about yourself, too. And maybe the hardest part to accept is that your parents were quite willing to see you go into this profession. In fact, they encouraged you. The very arms that nurtured you thrust you into the fatal clasp of pleasure seekers; the stranglehold of guilt on them must now be suffocating.

Priya: How could we all have been so foolish, so insane?

Jesus: That's the deceit of the human heart...and of the evil one. He enticed you, as he entices everyone, in small increments. It happens all too often.

You know, when the imagination is beguiled—which is where it all begins—and the will succumbs, the mind is unwittingly taken prisoner. With each breakdown of the will comes a greater imprisonment of the mind. You end up doing what you don't want to do, and not doing what you should do. How wretched you feel then!

Priya: In defense of my parents, I must say that this is the way it is in our small towns, Sir. Many parents send their daughters into this trade. I'm not excusing them, but I suppose it's all a matter of making a living. I don't know. There's much I don't understand anymore.

Jesus: It's not just *your* culture and *your* small towns, Priya. Gaining the world and losing the soul has been a malady of all mankind from the time people first tried to build names for themselves. There was a way that appeared right to you and your parents, as it does to every man and woman, but in the end it has brought you death—yes, even spiritual death.

You now know that you sought fulfillment for your hungers in the wrong places. I've said it many times: Man cannot live by bread alone, but by every word that proceeds from the mouth of God.

Priya: Those are strange words to me.

Jesus: I know they are. But I'd like to help you understand what they mean. I want to give you life and forgiveness, a promise for a better tomorrow, so that even though your body might wither and die, you will still live.

Buddha: I cannot remain silent anymore, Jesus. You've already said more than I can accept without interrupting. I, too, feel compassion for this woman, and I don't want her distracted by the things you're suggesting. Spiritual death, the Word of God, forgiveness—those are crutches for the spiritually weak. They're not realities but illusions!

And as for the evil one having some part here, I no longer believe these things in my enlightened condition. Only the immature or the uninformed cling to such mistruths. I'm sorry

Trying to reach for an
answer in this karmic cycle
is like putting your hand in
a bucket of glue and then
trying to wipe it clean.

to be so forthright, but we must seek the truth and do away with falsehood.

Jesus: Actually, I was wondering how long you'd remain silent. Your forthrightness is most welcome, Gautama. And your followers well know that debate and disagreement aren't exactly unfamiliar terrain to you. I'm certain you'll have much to say here. But I do have a plea. We've both said that truth must be pursued to wherever it leads—I assume you mean that to include both word and deed.

Buddha: Very much so.

My entire life was shaped by issues such as these. And I certainly debated them roundly with my opponents.

As you know, Jesus, I lived in a palace from my birth. I know that wealth and plenty don't satisfy—on that point I agree with you. Priya should've known this was so since her family is familiar with all of my teachings.

But all these things do not satisfy for a very different reason than the one you are ascribing, Jesus. I saw heartrending sights when I was young, and I was overcome with compassion. I can explain what this woman is going through.

Woman, you don't realize it, but everything you've lived through is the fruit of all that you yourself have sown. You were not free from debt when you were born, and you won't be free from debt when you die. You were born with a cup half full;

you have filled it the rest of the way. And your every act, word, and deed has to be paid for.

Jesus: Has to be paid for? Look at the masses alongside these shores—harried, preoccupied, all busy trying to earn a living. Carved into their consciences is this enormous moral debt you speak of. What an unbearable burden you're laying upon humanity, Gautama!

How does one pay? *With what* does one pay? And *to whom* does one pay? The creditor haunts but isn't there.

Buddha: But I didn't just arbitrarily make up this philosophy. Years of thought went into it. Where do I begin to explain it?

I'll grant you that this entanglement from past choices isn't an easy grip from which to free oneself. And looking at Priya, here, one groans under the burden.

But I have found a way. And that's the beauty. I've repeated that answer so many times.

Let me explain something to both of you. A moral law of cause and effect exists in the human consciousness. This has nothing to do with God or the evil one. Whether they exist or not is completely immaterial. The collective moral capital with which you were born, Priya, is something you had nothing to do with—that, at least, should bring you comfort.

But your present moral bankruptcy is because of the way you spent your life—that should bring you responsibility. You came into being bearing another's debt. Your choice was to reduce that debt or to pay it.

The word is *karma*—the karma of lives gone by and your own karma. This combination of what is inherited and what is spent is like a wheel that will either crush you or enable you to break free from its repetition when you've lived a pure life. You won't escape the results of what you've done.

There's hope, though! The sum of your good deeds and bad deeds will reappear in another life. You've made your deposit into an account that will be drawn from in a reborn life.

Priya: So I'll be reincarnated with another chance at payment, right?

Buddha: Not quite as simple as that. You're mistakenly using the term *reincarnated*. You're not technically *incarnated again*...you're *reborn* because you don't return as yourself. Another life will make its entrance after you're gone. That's the difference between what I call "rebirth" and what the Hindus call "reincarnation." I teach that another consciousness with the moral deposit reaped from your indebtedness will be born.

Priya: This is perplexing. It is at once my greatest hope and my greatest puzzle. My friends and I have often talked about this. Whose karma is being worked out when each life is wrapped around so many? I wonder: Are my parents also paying for past lives through my tragedy? Are my customers paying when I sell my diseased body to them? What about the baby that I gave up? Was that its karma, even before it knew anything about good or bad? I mean, trying to reach for an answer in this karmic cycle is like putting your hand in a bucket of glue and then trying to wipe it clean. Everything you touch becomes sticky and there's nowhere to wash it off.

Buddha: I have a technical term for all this: dependent origination. Your origin is dependent upon innumerable causes, Priya.

But that's far too complex to go into right now, and frankly, you must forget the past. There's nothing you can do to change that. And don't think of the future; it's all speculation. Deal only with the now. Free yourself now from the illusions of God and forgiveness and individual life hereafter. Invest in a life of good deeds that will outweigh the bad ones. That's your only hope. Make your heart pure, and that will offset all of your impure acts and thoughts.

Jesus: Well, Gautama, I can see that this discussion is going to take us far afield. Perhaps since Priya wants nothing more than answers to life itself, she won't mind if you and I talk as she listens in. But let's be sure that we get back at the end to what she personally needs to know. And by the way, Priya, you said it well: glue on the hands with nowhere to wash.

Buddha: Jesus, I must say a couple of things right now. The first is awkward, but it's better said right at the onset.

Those who define truth
by the calendar
run afoul of Him
who created time.

After my enlightenment I didn't let my disciples call me Gautama. It isn't proper to call one who has reached this stage by his common name. I'll let *you* do so, however, out of my respect for you. But I will not grant Priya that option. You see, I'm technically Gautama, the Buddha. I've reached the pinnacle of all knowledge and wisdom.

The second thing is that I will be most happy to talk on a range of issues with you. But you see, Jesus, even in what you just said, you were misleading Priya. My early followers made the same mistake you're making. You said that we must get back to dealing with what she "personally needs "…that's one of the core differences between you and me. This idea of "personal" is a delusion. If you don't mind, I'd like to retrace my spiritual journey to help you understand what I mean. I will then give you a hearing, as I've always taught that one ought to respect other religions.

Jesus: A point of clarification, though. It's true that you repeatedly called for the respect of all religions. But you also warned your followers to reject the falsehood in these religions. Although you were born a Hindu, didn't you reject some Hindu doctrines because you had some deep differences?

Buddha: Yes, but maybe we can pick that up later. I can see I'll have to be very careful with my words here.

As I was saying, I was comfortably situated in life. I had three palaces, one for each season. Stop me if you already know all this.

Jesus: Well, I do, and actually more than you realize, but I think it's good for Priya to hear it from you.

Buddha: I lived in a happy household with a host of material comforts. My parents gave me a very sheltered life. Actually, just seven days after I was born my mother died and I was raised by my aunt, whom my father married after the death of my mother. While still quite young, I married my cousin Yasodhara. She was a devoted wife. My parents had great hopes for us, and they wanted me to be shielded from all pain and suffering.

Ah! There's a key word, Jesus: *suffering!* Long before you came into this world—to be precise, over five centuries before you were born—I wrestled with this issue. The answer to this problem became the ultimate quest of my life.

Jesus: Your pursuit has obviously inspired your followers. But I think it's important that before you proceed we lay to rest this notion of "long before I was born."

Centuries before pain and suffering became your pursuit, one of the patriarchs of old, a man by the name of Job, wrestled with it night and day. I'm not sure you've even heard of him. In fact, Priya, I should add that he suffered even though he was a morally upright man. You can imagine *his* soul search in trying to figure it all out.

The answer he found was drastically different than yours,

How can time argue
with eternity?

Gautama. And in his story, Satan played a pivotal role—even as he did in yours, your discomfort with the idea of the evil one notwithstanding.

Buddha: This must've happened long before my time, because I haven't heard of Job.

Jesus: And if we must talk about who predates whom, another of my choice servants was Abraham, who also lived long before you. He lived to be a very old man, and I know the infirmities of old age particularly troubled you. But just when Abraham thought life was over, God birthed a miracle. Modern history and some of its anguish harkens back to what happened in Abraham's household.

I say all that just to say this: Abraham came more than a thousand years before you. And just for the record, before Abraham was, I Am.

That is why John the Baptizer, who announced my coming, said of me, "There comes one after me who is greater than me because he was before me."

So time ought not to be a factor of seniority here, if you don't mind. Those who define truth by the calendar run afoul of Him who created time.

Buddha: That was quite a response, Jesus! I must take note of it because my followers do pride themselves in dating my earthly sojourn before yours. But I see your point: How can time argue with eternity?

Anyhow, over the course of my life, I saw many sights that distressed me greatly. Old age (as you pointed out)! My, how that troubled me. To see a body wasting away over time gives one pause. But all that paled when I considered the next sight: death! What a morbid, painful reality.

Then the third, sickness! Disease. Pain. How can we be rid of them?

All these stirred me beyond words. I couldn't live without facing the anguish of these realities. I knew I had to leave my home to find an explanation for these mysteries.

As I pondered that, I saw a wandering ascetic living a life of scant provision. Maybe that's the answer, I thought. I should do the same.

When my father heard that I was planning to leave, he shook like a tree struck by an elephant, and in a voice choked with tears, he pleaded with me not to go. I had no choice but to leave home and find the answer. Yes, I left my wife Yasodhara, and I left the very night our son was born. I named him Rahula, which means "fetters" or "shackles," because he was an encumbrance to my pursuit of peace. Wife, children, parents—all were an attachment that I had to leave if I was to find true peace.

Priya: I've always admired you for that, O venerable one!

Buddha: I didn't do it to be admired. I did it because I was in search of answers.

When you mix falsehood
with truth,
you create a more
destructive lie.

My first path was the way of the ascetic. I labored at that for six long years. I ate hardly anything, starving my body in search of the self. I followed the teachings of the Hindu sages because, as you said, I was born a Hindu and had studied under two great Brahman teachers. But it brought me no peace. Hinduism didn't have the answers. Among other doctrines, I disagreed with the authority of the Vedas, to which Hindus subscribe. I know that didn't sit comfortably with my Hindu friends, but so it was. In fact, anytime my followers are uncomfortable with some of my teachings, they blame it on some Hindu influence I hadn't completely shaken off. I find that a trifle humorous!

Anyhow, I resolved that I was not going to give up my personal pursuit. I had lived a life of intense sacrifice and was reduced to a shell of a body. My spine stood out like a corded rope, my ribs projected like the jutting rafters of an old, roofless cowshed, and the light of my eyes, sunk down in their sockets, looked like the gleam of water in a deep well. I didn't realize what lay ahead of me. I was asleep to my own destiny.

Then in one stretch of several days I sat motionless under a fig tree in a place called Bodhgaya. As I was meditating, something strange and wonderful happened. There came upon me a transcending memory of all my thousands—indeed, infinite number—of previous lives, and everything past, present, and future opened up like a book before me. I was in a state of unparalleled tranquillity. I would call it a life of perfect balance.

It was as if light and its absence commingled. I saw as I had never seen before. I saw the illusion with which humanity lives. At the same time, something was extinguished as it had never been extinguished before. Every passion, every craving, every desire was gone. I was unmoved by either joy or sorrow. I became unshackled from desire. I was at peace with reality and needed nothing in any way, shape, or form. I was now the Buddha—the Enlightened One.

Jesus: You determined not to give up your *personal* pursuit, did you say?

Buddha: Now, now, before you say anything to confuse this, may I add something here? I was concerned with one fundamental matter—Truth. I have since told my disciples never to follow anything or anyone just because somebody else says so. You must taste and see for yourself whether something is true or false. To that I am firmly committed.

Jesus: "Unshackled from desire." What a statement, Gautama! "Extinguishing all hungers." An incredible ideal. Just think about it. How can it be possible that *all* desires are wrong? That issue alone could dominate our discussion, couldn't it?

There's so much to say, yet one cannot bear it all at once. But let me say that you remind me of another I once saw under a fig tree. His story is told in the Gospels. His name was Nathanael, which means "gift of God"—now there's another great name, Priya!

Well, the first time I saw him, to his utter surprise I called him by name. He wondered how I even knew him. Then, to add to his shock, I revealed to him the innermost inclinations of his heart. He was dumbfounded. He had come with his prejudices, thinking there was no new truth that someone from Nazareth could give to him because Nazareth was the lowliest of all towns. (That, by the way, is my home city, Gautama.)

Yet when Nathanael and I had finished talking, he had had a glimpse of heaven itself. Few experiences are as jolting as really knowing yourself for the first time through meeting someone else. That's the power and unpretentiousness of truth.

Priya: I've never heard of any of these stories, Jesus.

Jesus: You'll hear a few more before we're finished.

Anyhow, Gautama, whatever happened as you meditated under the tree is the story of your life. Your heart of compassion is proverbial. You were willing to give up all the comforts this world affords.

In fact, even as I observe your followers, they work hard at being compassionate and selfless. Some of my followers can learn much from their simplicity.

But something else quickly stands out: rules, scores of rules, like a noose tauntingly swaying above the head, ready at the hint of one wrong move to be tightened around the neck. I see all the laws of conduct written in various centers of your teaching.

Take a look at this catalog of rules by which one builds his merit: 4 sets of rules for 4 great offenses, 13 rules required for formal participation in the brotherhood, 30 rules to curb greed and possessions, 92 rules of offenses under yet another category, 75 rules for proper behavior of novices who seek admission to the order, and 7 ways of settling disputes.

The list goes on—227 rules for the male monk and 311 for the female—plus scores of fine-print contingencies. This is the Rule Book of rule books!

I see the wandering monks with their bowls in their hands, beginning each day with the hope of bringing themselves under these precepts, none ever quite sure if they've made it. It's quite a life they lead, set apart from the mainstream.

Boat Driver: May I dare to add something funny here? Yesterday's paper had a picture of one of the monks in the monastery on his cell phone! I thought that was—

Buddha: Please! Let's stay on course and not get into all that.

Boat Driver: I'm sorry.

Jesus: The fact is that countless numbers have sought the way of renunciation. Some have sat in caves for a lifetime in meditative silence. I see them even now. I hear them in their wordless cries—but Gautama, you've not seen their hearts as I have.

Priya: I've heard about them in other lands. Are you talking about some of those in the caves of Tibet who've been alone in

Morality as a badge of attainment breeds the deadliest state of mind—a delusion of absolute autonomy.

meditation for ten, fifteen years, and...I mean, how can they do that? If that's what it takes—scores of rules for some, silence for decades for others—what chance do I have?

Jesus. A better chance than you realize, Priya, but I don't want to interrupt Buddha's train of thought. It's important that you hear what he has to offer you.

We haven't yet reached the core of your thinking, Gautama. Mere renunciation isn't enough, and you know that well. You discovered that asceticism didn't bring the answer. Abraham, too, left everything he had in search of a city that would be eternal. My choice servant, Moses, considered the pleasures of a palace not something to be possessed and left it to suffer along with his people. One of the most powerful shapers of the New Testament church was the apostle Paul. He was willing to treat as dirt every credential that his people considered worth possessing. In fact, I myself did not consider my equality with God something to be grasped but stripped myself of any reputation and came to earth in the form of a servant.

You're offering nothing unique. Many other religions boast notable martyrs for their causes. Hindus, Muslims, and, yes, even atheists. So the mere fact of renunciation isn't enough, is it?

Buddha: No. But I came to a different conclusion than they did.

Jesus: You most certainly did. But let's examine it.

You said that when you were enlightened you came to a realization you had never experienced before, including the awareness of an infinite number of previous lives. Tell us more about this since that defines the ultimate destiny you beckon everyone to. There's so much talk about nirvana and yet so little understanding of it.

Buddha: Unfortunately, that is true. Just read the books about it. Talk about confusion! One of the reasons is that people don't understand death.

Jesus: I must agree with you on that!

Buddha: But I might also add that your life, Jesus, has shown the most exemplary qualities one could want to see. In fact, many of my followers have written about how close your teachings are to mine. Some of them have even called us brothers, and may be surprised to envision a conversation between us that would draw out any differences.

Jesus: But, sad to say, those very scholars have taken the lighter matters of what I taught and have neglected the weightier matters at the heart of my teaching.

When you mix falsehood with truth, you create a more destructive lie. In fact, many of those very scholars have even distorted what you have taught. You know, Gautama, morality as a badge of attainment breeds the deadliest state of mind—a delusion of absolute autonomy.

Prayer in its most basic
form is the surging
of the human spirit
in its weakness, grasping
at the Spirit of God
in His strength.

A young ruler, also very rich, once came to me and told me that he had kept all the moral precepts, yet was still looking for life. It had eluded him, even though he had circumspectly kept the moral law.

By contrast, one who sees his or her spiritual poverty and comes to God for help is far closer to God's kingdom. It's a bit like standing on a mountain and looking down at a city below. If the only path down the mountain winds around it, at times you may actually find yourself farther from the city, sometimes even losing sight of it, in order to get closer to the city.

The morally confident person demeans the distance and loses the path. The impoverished in spirit, humbled by the distance, keeps to the path and reaches the goal. That's why, Priya, you may be closer to the kingdom than you think, and I will show you the way.

Priya: Your illustrations are compelling, Jesus. You read my heart well. I'm listening.

Jesus: I would like you to continue, Gautama.

Buddha: Yes, yes, and I hope we get back to those issues, too. I was saying that I saw life as I'd never seen it before. First and foremost, life is suffering. I call this *Dukkha*, a word incorporating the breadth of human agony. This isn't just the simple idea of pain. This is an all-encompassing sense of life lived with perpetual loss. All of life's aches, hurts, and longings. This is suffering.

Then I saw the cause of suffering. All suffering is caused by longing, by desire, by attachment. That was so plain to see.

Next came the answer to end suffering. And for that I conceived the eightfold path that leads to nirvana.

These four stages—suffering, the cause of suffering, the end of suffering, and the eightfold path—I called the four noble truths.

But here again I have to be careful to explain every stage. For example, when I say "cause of suffering," I struggle for words, because suffering doesn't have a singular cause. No one cause stands alone. There are a number of causes woven into this tangled web, which we cannot unravel thread by thread.

If I were to take two words to summarize the dilemma of being human, they would be *ignorance* and *craving*. Take Priya, for example. I pity her very much, but her life-destroying error lay in her ignorance of who she really is, not just in her existence but in her essence. In that ignorance, thinking she was pleasing herself, she went hungering after money, comfort, and success, and now she lies here shattered and dying…and she has taken others with her. Had she been devoid of her "self" and her victims devoid of their "selves," this would never have happened.

Jesus: Fascinating! Here we approach the first major point of surface similarity but substantive difference. When you say that

God answers every
prayer by either giving
what is asked for or
reminding the petitioner
that God's provision
is built on His wisdom
and executed in His time.

she needs to free herself from the idea of self, there's a world of difference between what you're meaning and what *I* mean when I say that one must deny himself before following me.

Buddha: Yes, that's true, and I hesitate to say much more because, as you know, Jesus, after I realized enlightenment, I actually thought of spending my life without uttering a word of what I'd found. I was convinced that my discovery was unique and to most people unfathomable. But I broke my silence partly because my followers assured me that I was wrong in my appraisal that they wouldn't be able to understand the truth of my realizing nirvana.

But I continue to believe that these concepts are lofty and difficult to explain. So how much can this woman understand, I still question? But this much she must understand: that she has to shake off this notion of a personal self. You're hoping we get back to her personal quest, Jesus, but I hope exactly the opposite. I hope that she will bury that personal pursuit once and for all.

Jesus: Whatever else people may say of your teaching, Gautama, they cannot accuse you of not thinking about life's problems.

You've talked about our ignorance in thinking we have a self, and you've also said you were reluctant to teach it at first, until your audience prevailed. I agree with at least one of the reasons. You cannot pour new wine into old wineskins.

Buddha: Frankly, I'm a little uncomfortable with that metaphor, because my followers are prohibited from consuming alcohol.

Jesus: Would you prefer that I say "You cannot take a patch of new cloth and sew it onto an old garment"?

Buddha: I really like that.

Boat Driver: My clothes prove it.

Priya: Yes, I noticed.

Jesus: But there's something deeper in your change of thought, Gautama, and I think it's important that we pursue it. You say that you had reached a place of perfect knowledge and understanding; yet you were *corrected* by your disciples, not merely on the timing, but on the very mission you ultimately set upon. Please tell me, doesn't that sound a bit odd?

Light and darkness had commingled. Tranquillity was perfect. Knowledge was complete. No more desire. Yet the "unenlightened" were able to correct the "enlightened" and change your conclusion…and you condescended? I'm not sure it makes sense. Can you explain a little more about how you, who claimed to know all, were persuaded to change your mind? And there were numerous other serious matters on which you yielded to their pressure.

Buddha: Yes, that's true. Long after my enlightenment my father came to me and requested that no young person join my

In persistent, fervent prayer, God prepares the soil of one's heart to make room for the seed of His answer, from which will flower an alignment with His will.

ranks without parental permission. He had a reason for that, of course: because I had left home without his permission. So I made that a precondition for any young man who wanted to join my ranks.

As for my stepmother...well, that's another story! She came to me three times and pleaded to be allowed into the ranks of the monks, and I didn't permit her to do so because I was uncertain about women being in the order. I felt it wasn't possible for women to really pay the price. Then she, along with several hundred women, shaved their heads and came once again, this time represented by my disciple Ananda, who persuaded me to accept them by reminding me of how she had sacrificially taken care of me. I finally relented and admitted them. I suppose these are the things you're thinking of.

But Jesus, my followers have pointed out how God, too, changed His mind at the entreaty of Moses or Abraham. So what's the difference?

Jesus: There is a fundamental difference, Gautama. And for Priya's sake, I truly hope this is understood.

As I pointed out earlier, one of the biggest mistakes people make is to see a small point of similarity and forget the world of difference behind it. They end up straining out a gnat and swallowing a camel.

Buddha: That metaphor stirs my eastern mind with delight! Please continue.

Jesus: You see, Gautama, God has given His followers the privilege of prayer and intercession. Prayer is a constant reminder that the human being is not autonomous. Prayer in its most basic form is the surging of the human spirit in its weakness, grasping at the Spirit of God in His strength. Sometimes mere words cannot give shape to the longing of the heart. You see, Gautama, God answers every prayer by either giving what is asked for or reminding the petitioner that God's provision is built on His wisdom and executed in His time. But the answer is always for the instruction and nurture of the soul. Never is any new knowledge added to the mind of God.

God doesn't respond because someone opens up some new insight for Him. No. In persistent, fervent prayer, God prepares the soil of one's heart to make room for the seed of His answer, from which will flower an alignment with His will.

That's why I often told my disciples to be persistent and pray in faith. When the seed meets the soil and the season is right, the bloom touches heaven.

Buddha: Beautifully put. But prayer is a dimension that doesn't fit in with my teaching.

Jesus: Exactly! And this is the point. When *you* changed your mind, it wasn't because something had changed in the petitioner; something had changed in *you.* You drastically altered the very makeup of your following because you were moved from a place of disbelieving something to believing it.

Whom did the LORD consult to enlighten him, and who taught him the right way?

That's the reason I was careful to say that your disciples were able to change your assumptions and your conclusions—not the form, but the very substance.

That is never true of God, who knows the beginning from the end. A plea for mercy does not diminish God's perfect knowledge. In fact, it is part of the very pattern God has designed for responding to the sincere heart.

Priya: I passionately want to understand this, Jesus. I really do. How often I dreamed that my prayer—that my cry—was heard by some power greater than mine.

Jesus: Isn't this also a core difference, Gautama? Just as the call of karma demands payment of a debt when there is no creditor to receive it, so with the desire of your followers to make a petition for their needs, there is no one to whom they can go.

My prophet Isaiah talks of a man who went to sleep hungry. He dreamed during the night that he was at a banquet, feasting, only to wake up and find out it was a dream.

Your followers meditate, they chant, they try to empty their minds of all desire; yet how does prayer slip in when there is no God to pray to?

Buddha: Yes, there are cardinal differences between one who prays and one who meditates. One looks beyond and the other looks within. And it's true that with my followers prayer does "slip in," as you say. That's when reason is set aside and emotion triumphs.

May I backtrack for a moment? There's at least a partial explanation for why I made some changes. But frankly, I don't want to get into all that because it's beside the point, Jesus. People make more of this than I intended. As you know, some of my followers have quarreled over this for centuries.

The truth is that I lived for forty-five years after realizing nirvana before my parinirvana, my departure into oblivion, at death. But during those forty-five years there was a process of clarification for me. All understanding takes time. And I was no different.

Jesus: I'm not much interested in the particulars either. I only raised the point because there's much more at stake here than just clarification.

You see, Gautama, you made it very clear when you met your followers, long after you realized nirvana, that you needed no teacher. You made a major point of this, that you were taught by no one, that you were dependent upon no one, that your realization was completely self-caused and self-realized—just as Priya's condition, you said, is self-caused and needs only the self to correct. Nothing more, no one else.

You were emphatic that there was no need for God to explain the created order and no need for God to be your teacher. You said repeatedly that each person was his or her own refuge. Yet it's evident there was so much you still did not know. Your admission I respect; your reasoning on this doesn't comport with reality.

There are mysteries to life that are still beyond you, yet you claim to have arrived. Is this not troublesome to you?

Buddha: No, because I believe I *have* arrived.

Jesus: How do you break free from the tension? You insist on the pursuit of truth wherever it leads but get snared by this breakdown in your own claim. You not only claimed to know everything, but you also said that you knew even more than God. Job thought he knew everything, too, and when God confronted him with a flurry of questions, Job was thoroughly embarrassed about how much he did not know. He realized as never before that all knowledge ultimately belongs to God, not to man.

Three centuries before you came on the scene, my prophet Isaiah said:

> Who has understood the mind of the LORD,
> or instructed him as his counselor?
> Whom did the LORD consult to enlighten him,
> and who taught him the right way?...
> To whom, then, will you compare God?
> What image will you compare him to?
> Do you not know?
> Have you not heard?
> The LORD is the everlasting God,
> the Creator of the ends of the earth.
> He will not grow tired or weary,
> and his understanding no one can fathom.

That is the same God who will say to Priya in her broken condition,

> "I give strength to the weary and increase
> the power of the weak.
> Even youths grow tired and weary,
> and young men stumble and fall;
> but those who hope in the LORD
> will renew their strength.
> They will soar on wings like eagles;
> they will run and not grow weary,
> they will walk and not be faint."

I know the number of hairs on your head, Priya. I know when every sparrow falls to the ground. I intimately know and care about how your heart aches. I even knew you before you came to be.

In fact, we will see how inescapable these truths are even among your followers, Gautama.

I would love to pursue this a bit, but I must wait awhile. I know you wish to complete the thought on this "illusion" of self that your enlightenment dispelled.

Buddha: It's my turn to say, "Fascinating." I've always appreciated an inquiring mind and I will be eager to hear. However, I'm beginning to feel a bit uneasy in that I'm answering all your

You cannot reconstitute
reality just by
changing language.

questions and haven't had a chance to pose any to you. I certainly hope I will get the chance.

Jesus: You will. But when I began, you said you weren't comfortable with this woman being led astray, so I thought it would be good to hear what you *do* consider the truth.

Buddha: Fair enough. But I'll have my chance too, right?

Jesus: Anytime you're ready, just say so.

Buddha: All right. It won't be long, I can assure you. You were asking...oh yes! About the self. You see, the self that we claim is actually nonexistent. It exists nowhere, neither in our physicality nor in our mental parts.

Look at this boat. Is it the wood? Is it the motor? Is it the glue? Is it the paint? No, it's none of these. In the same way, the self does not exist in any of the individual elements that we are composed of, nor is it outside of them. We're nothing more than physical quantities, and when that physical being dies, the individual dies as well. Nothing remains beyond that consciousness. And all of our troubles begin by having this sense that there's an individual, united self.

It's only when you realize that the self doesn't exist and that you're living with an illusion of self that suffering comes to an end.

All of this woman's desires were for her self. Take a look at this pathetic, shriveled-up body that Priya lives with. If she had seen that she didn't have a self, she would've stopped trying to satisfy that self and would never have entered into this state of devastation.

Once we realize that the self doesn't exist, we find the middle way between asceticism and pleasure, and in that balance, life ceases to hold us hostage to our attachments.

Jesus: Gautama, your plea is puzzling. I really wanted to interrupt you earlier, but I held my tongue!

First you told us that there is no God. Then you said that you know more than God. You've also said that when "gods" come to the realization that you have, they will be promoted to your state. You went on to postulate a moral law apart from God and to assert that each one owes a moral debt flowing within "the human stream of consciousness," whatever that means. *Now we're told that there is no such person as Priya.*

No real self on the one hand—but her self is all she needs, on the other hand, to find the truth? What does all this mean?

Listen to your own words; they speak a different message: "Once *we* realize... *We* find the middle way... If *she* only knew... *She* would not be... Life ceases to hold *us.*"

All these assume personality, Gautama. *Who* are *we* talking about? This *you* and *she* are particular individuals, not to be confused with any other *him* or *her.* You cannot shake off the person no matter how hard you try. And it stands to reason. You cannot reconstitute reality just by changing language.

It's not so much the
illusion of self but the self
over God that breeds a
breakdown of what God
intended us to be.

Priya: It does seem confusing to say there is no self, yet I'm all I need to solve my problem. I don't understand this. I'm not sure I'm saying it well. You both are better at words than I am.

Jesus: Oh no, you're saying it very well.

My assertion is that each one *is* an individual—created unique and created in the image of God. That's why your analogy of the boat, Gautama, should be a contrast, not a comparison. There's no breath in it. It's but a thing that man has carved with his own hands.

You didn't turn to the boat for wisdom or understanding. I'll grant you that there is a plan, a design—and a designer. That's why it steers and floats. But it's lifeless. When this boat is old and decaying, you won't be sitting here explaining to it the tragedy of being old.

Boat Driver: I hope it doesn't get old too soon. I haven't finished paying for it yet.

Jesus: Thank you, Driver....

But when you see Priya, Gautama, you're not seeing a boat or just a thing to be used. You see why even God is mindful of her. He has made her less than a god and crowned her with dignity and honor. In her being she reflects what it means to be made in God's image. In her present state she grieves the loss of that dignity. That's why she wrestles with such lofty ideas. Even her misery is a veiled reflection of her grandeur.

Buddha: Here we part most seriously, Jesus. Why do we need God to have that dignity? I gave humanity rules and laws for their dignity. Well, maybe we'd better not get into that till we deal with this "self" a bit more. I think I may have interrupted you.

Jesus: No, that's all right. But a thought or two might help.

It's surprising that you haven't yet discerned that morality itself cannot bring freedom or dignity, Gautama. Extremism toward moral claims is the chronic bent of the human mind. Some take moral precepts and apply them with ruthless rigor. They pile law upon law till they break under the burden of legalism. Others try to escape from that burden by seeking unbridled pleasure. As we lift our eyes from this boat, we see the ascetic and the indulgent. This is nothing new.

When my servant John the Baptist lived in the wilderness, many lashed out at his rigorous pursuit of the law. When I ate and drank with the moral rejects of society, the moralizers called me a glutton and a drunkard. Just as the lack of wisdom in a parent is lived out in the child, so every generation without God, bereft of wisdom, will have opposing reactions to moral issues.

Isn't that the first clue to finding an answer for the source of human dignity? It's not so much the illusion of self but the *self over God* that breeds a breakdown of what God intended us to be.

Buddha: I must admit that I've never gotten into a discussion this profound before. In fact, some of my disciples that I discussed these issues with were pretty pathetic in their understanding of such things. Nevertheless, I do have a response, but please finish the thought.

Jesus: I'll just say that your espousal of an absence of self is the most unique and fearsome claim you made, a concept that cuts across virtually every major belief. You turned from Hinduism because it said there was an essential self, which they called the *atman*. And on that denial you hung everything else.

At the heart of the Mosaic law were the commands to love the Lord your God with all your heart, soul, and strength, and to love your neighbor as yourself. These were God's greatest commandments, and on them hung all the Law and the prophets.

My invitation to each person is to deny himself before he begins to follow me. But your response is that there is no self to deny.

Buddha: And that when you realize this, all suffering ceases.

Jesus: I would suggest to you, Gautama, that in looking for an answer to suffering, you haven't dealt with the problem of suffering at all—you've just tried to obliterate relationships. We think of ourselves as an "I," but you say there is no "I."

Wasn't that the very reason your father pleaded that you

not allow young people to follow you without parental permission—because he was going to lose his next son from the household too? He had a particular love for a particular life. He couldn't just dismiss it as mere consciousness.

Isn't this the very reason Priya's parents grieve right now?

Take her hand, Gautama, and see that you're not touching just skin and bones, but a person.

Buddha: No, I cannot touch her.

Jesus: That's the ultimate expression of her destitution.

You heard what she said. Her parents gave her this cherished name because to them she wasn't just a stream of consciousness. Or must we tell them that if they weren't attached to her, they wouldn't grieve? What you've lost in denying the self as real is not the problem of pain but the essence of being.

A group of Sadducees once came to me and asked about a woman who had married seven times. They wanted to know which of those men would be her husband in heaven. They didn't believe in resurrection from the dead, and so by posing this question, they thought they were disproving the resurrection.

You're in a similar situation. You seek to solve the problem of suffering, and in order to solve it, you say that the self doesn't exist. This attachment to detachment and the expulsion of the self only opens the door to further questions that are even more difficult to answer.

Love is particular...

that's why each

one has a name.

Buddha: Yes, Jesus, there is a world of difference in our views on this matter. And I'm thinking even as I speak. You see, a lotus flower goes through several stages of development. In one it lies buried under the water as a young plant. It has not yet seen the sun. In another it lies half submerged in the water, caught between two worlds of water and air. In a third it rises well above the water and blossoms in the full light of day.

That's the way we come to knowledge: in degrees. Someday you'll realize that the goodness of life is seen only when you break free from submersion in this doctrine of self.

Jesus: A boat! A lotus flower! Your metaphors lose the *person.* But speaking of submersion…

Driver, can you slow down a bit? You remind me of Jehu, the chariot driver in the narrative of the kings of Israel!

Thank you, Wat.

Boat Driver: I'm so sorry, Sir! I was preoccupied listening to this conversation. I certainly wouldn't want to risk the lives of such important people…. Oh, forgive me! Did I…did I say the wrong thing?

Priya: I would say so. Risking the life of someone who says he is the author of life? And forgiveness? We don't even know what that means.

Boat Driver: I guess I'd better stay quiet. And how did you know my name, Jesus?

Jesus: I thought you said you were listening very carefully to the conversation.

Boat Driver: I think I get it.

Jesus: That's good. I haven't forgotten you, Wat.

Gautama, I agree that there are stages we go through. I, too, had to wait before I fully disclosed who I was to my disciples. But that was because I knew what was in the hearts of men and women. They're fickle, and they follow for the wrong reason. I want to make this point very clear. I am like a shepherd who cares for his sheep, not wanting even one to be lost, because every one matters. Every one. This is so pivotal to my gospel.

Love is particular. God loves the world so that the "whosoevers" who believe in Him will not perish but have everlasting life. God loves every man, woman, and child as an individual. That's why each one has a name. If there were no particularities, the death of one wouldn't be a loss—each could easily be replaced by the birth of another.

But each one is unique, and it's only when they find me as their Savior that they are able to give full expression to their uniqueness. The path of that person then begins like the first gleam of dawn, shining brighter to the full light of day.

Boat Driver: That's a beautiful picture, Jesus, especially for a boatman who starts his day early.

The path of that person
then begins like the
first gleam of dawn,
shining brighter to
the full light of day.

Buddha: Not just for boatmen, but for anyone in the dark...that's why I speak of enlightenment.

Jesus: Ah, but there's the catch: You have to explain to this woman what you mean when you say that she's not an individual and that she burns from full candlelight to the "extinguishing of a candle." That's nirvana, at which point there will be no such person as Priya.

But I say to her, "Come to me, you who struggle and are weighed down, and you will find rest in your very soul. Take my yoke upon you and learn from me, for I am gentle and humble in heart, and you will find rest for your soul. Before you were born I knew you and have loved you with an everlasting love. I came looking for you, to save you. Cast your cares upon me, Priya, for I care for you. In fact, if you were to die today, you could be with me in paradise."

Gautama, I am the Light of the world—Priya will see life's purpose because of me. I am the Bread of Life—she will be full because of me. I am the Good Shepherd—she will be guided by me. Without me, nothing was ever made that was made—she is known because of me. I laid down my life for her—she will be forgiven because of me. There never was a time when I was not, and there will never be a time when I will not be—she will live because of me. These are credentials you have never claimed.

Buddha: With all due respect, Jesus, how can you make such claims? And I repeat my objection: Why is God necessary for us to know who we are? I think I'm ready to start asking you the questions.

Jesus: I would be pleased to answer them. I've obviously touched a nerve. But do you mind if we get off here for a few minutes? I see an enormous temple over there, and I think I can answer your questions as we walk through it.

Here, Priya, let me give you a hand. You're very weak, and I will stay close to you.

Buddha: I'm not sure I like everything I see here, Jesus, I must admit. These temples have become puzzling places for me. I didn't want to be deified or made into a statue. The gold, the precious stones, all on a carved idol...

Jesus: Walking into the temple in Jerusalem and seeing what I saw was not my favorite moment, either.

Priya: Did we lose our driver? I thought he was coming.

Jesus: He stopped to light some incense. Can you see him? There he is...chanting a prayer.

Buddha: This is precisely what I mean. I don't understand how all this ritual and idolatry has come about. I told my followers not to be burdened with images and with worship, but they didn't listen. What I taught and what has become of what I taught are two different things.

Jesus: That seems to be the inevitable result when someone assigns themselves authority over the intent of someone else's thoughts or words. My people also turned their backs on me and polluted the worship of the true God. But there's a difference between the two, even here.

Priya: Please explain.

Jesus: Think about these two words, *superstition* and *legalism.* They end up looking the same but are born out of different sentiments.

Superstition in its essence is actually a subtle lack of faith in God. If there is no righteous God in control of all things, a person ends up trying to appease the world of unseen power. Habits develop out of fear of the unknown. You took God away from them, Gautama, so they live in fear of the spirit world. Anytime God is displaced but belief in the spirit world remains, placation will dominate the individual's efforts.

The corruption that attended *my* followers was the other side of the coin. When grace is evicted, laws or power-seeking people take over. Legalism enters and ceremony becomes the focus.

These two things—superstition and legalism—rush into hearts bereft of a God of mercy and grace.

Your followers are consumed with ritual and fear, and you don't recognize the cause.

Buddha: Those are strong words, Jesus.

Jesus: Let me demonstrate a simple fact here. Priya, why don't you invite that monk to join us for lunch?

Priya: But it's past twelve o'clock, Sir! These monks don't eat after the noon hour. He'll be violating his code of discipline. Besides, I'm a woman. I cannot place food directly into his hands.

Jesus: Wat, why don't you give him this fruit?

Boat Driver: You really want me to do that?

Jesus: Yes, I do.

Boat Driver: All right, I'll try…

Well, I offered it to him, Sir, and he refused. He said it would pollute him. But he allowed me to put it into his bag, so long as he didn't touch it.

Jesus: You see, Gautama, that's what I mean by legalism.

Now look at those people outside that spirit house nearby. Why did they build that spirit house, Priya?

Priya: Oh, we all do that. If we don't, some bad things could happen to us. So we bring offerings to appease departed spirits in the hope that no harm will come to us.

Anytime God is displaced
but belief in the spirit
world remains, placation
will dominate the
individual's efforts.

Buddha: But Jesus, this is all a corruption of what I taught.

Jesus: Maybe so, but let me trace the route of that corruption. First, you told them there is no God. Then you told them there is no self. You also told them there is no one to pray to. You told them there is no evil one to fear. You told them everything is only within themselves, even though those selves do not exist. You instructed them that their good deeds have to outweigh their bad deeds. You carved into their consciousness a huge debt. You gave them scores of rules to live by. You told them all desire is to be cut off. You told them you would cease to be, and, when they have paid, *they* will cease to be.

How can all this bring peace, Gautama? Think about it!

They cannot escape the conviction of a power greater than themselves. A sense of worship and awe is inextricably woven into the human condition. If they don't find it in spirit and in truth, they will find it in the flesh and in falsehood.

There is only one who offers solace and fulfillment in spirit and in truth...and that is God.

Buddha: There we go again.... God.

Jesus: And there you go again with your constant effort to do away with God. Gautama, may I ask you a simple philosophical question?

Buddha: Yes.

Jesus: You said you recalled an infinite number of births, didn't you?

Buddha: Yes.

Jesus: But you also had a final birth?

Buddha: Yes.

Jesus: How can an infinite number have finality?

Buddha: Shall we then call it numberless?

Jesus: You still have the same problem. You cannot evade this contradiction. That's why I began the first book of the Old Testament and one of the books of the New Testament with "In the beginning, God!" A quantity has limitations. An eternal, infinite being is not the same as a quantity.

Buddha: I'm thinking; keep talking.

Jesus: The same applies to morality. Morality is inextricably joined to personhood. There is no way to talk of what one *ought* to do without showing the value of the person. In fact, wasn't your objection to the caste system one of the reasons you rejected Hinduism?

Buddha: Yes.

Jesus: You saw the problem, but where's the solution? There's no way to confer value on a person unless that value is intrinsic. There's no way value can be intrinsic unless that person is created

There is no way to talk of
what one ought to do
without showing the value
of the person.

by one of ultimate worth. That's why the heart craves worship; it seeks "worthship" in the object that's revered.

The purpose in life, Gautama, is communion, not union. There can be no meaning when the goal is to meditate oneself into oblivion. But meaning is found in a relationship with the living God. That's what it's all about—a relationship. And *I* am the one who is the way, the truth, and the life. He who comes to me will be fulfilled. I work the miracle of extinguishing destructive hungers and planting new, legitimate hungers to take their place. I give to you life that's abundant. I offer a new relationship.

Buddha: Ah, but Jesus, haven't many in your name also perverted worship, even though you offered yourself, your person, to them?

Jesus: Yes, many have perverted the worship of the living God and continue to do so. But please take note of the difference: The entanglement of your followers in superstition was a logical departure from your teaching because there was no God to start with. Their hearts drove them to a transcendent one, but you said there was none to be found. The substitute was worship in any form.

The departure of *my* followers was inconsistent with my teaching because they *forgot* God. They replaced the well of God with broken cisterns of their own making.

Also, you told your followers that they had to go beyond you. So, in a sense, they went beyond you.

But the same cannot be said of God. There is no greater beyond.

Buddha: But a perversion is a perversion, isn't it? What difference does the nature of the perversion make?

Jesus: I knew that would be the question. We're almost back to where we began.

There is one major difference between your indictment of false worship and mine, a difference you cannot deny.

Wherever the worship of the living God has been perverted, it has always been the result of a departure from my Word. This is so important that I want to dwell on it for a moment. You see, one has to find out what is eternal and then interpret the true value of everything in that light.

I taught my disciples that though everything on earth would someday pass away, the Word that I gave to them remains forever. I told them that anyone who adds or takes away from this Word will be accursed. I told them that the Scriptures cannot be broken.

Right from the beginning, the greatest question ever asked was "Has God really spoken?" The answer to that is a resounding "Yes!" That's why I told Priya that it's not bread that we live by, but every word that comes from the mouth of God. When

If there is no
permanent truth,
even the statement
that everything is
impermanent is only
impermanently true.

my people depart from that Word, other hungers take charge. Individual lives become prostituted, and worship itself is prostituted.

Buddha: Well, I gave my disciples no written word as an abiding authority.

Jesus: Now we're getting somewhere, Gautama. Why didn't you give them an abiding authority?

Buddha: Because…everything is impermanent.

Jesus: Even that statement? Is that impermanent too?

Buddha: I think…I'll have to think on that. I have a terrible feeling I'm backing myself into a corner here.

Jesus: That's what I'm saying to you. Your followers have no final word to rely on. If there's no final word, how does one accuse another of "perversion"? In fact, some of your followers say that even if you had remained silent there would've been no loss of insight, as far as they're concerned.

There is no permanent truth if everything is impermanent. And even the statement that everything is impermanent is only impermanently true. Which means the absolute you posit becomes only relatively true. If it's only relatively true, it can no longer be stated as an absolute.

You see, you inadvertently proved that truth is asserted principally by words and can be tested by reason. How, then, do we know what is true if nothing is ever said or thought in assertions? And you have no eternally binding word.

Buddha: But everything else I have taught hangs on that statement of impermanence.

Jesus: I'll leave you to draw the inevitable conclusion. You did say that we ought to follow the truth wherever it leads?

Buddha: I did.

Jesus: May I finish by saying that when my people cast aside the Word, the absolute is lost? Pollution in worship is the result. Life's ultimate purpose is desecrated.

Buddha: Suppose I were to grant that, Jesus. Why on earth should we take *your* word to be the truth?

Jesus: I promised Priya that I would personalize the answer for her at the end. Maybe the time has come.

Priya, if there's any consolation, you're not alone in your situation. In my Word I tell the story of a woman who came to drink some water from a well. She had all kinds of questions about worship. But her real problem was that she had squandered the special person God made her to be. Numerous marriages had come and gone. She was a lonely woman. When I gave her my message of love and eternal life, she ran back to her village to tell the people that she had found the one who knew her frailties, yet loved her for who she was. For the first time she found worth. I *disclose* the heart of every person who comes to me. You, too, are special to me, Priya. I see your heart better than you can.

Priya: Can I read that story somewhere, Sir?

Jesus: Yes, it's in the Gospel of John.

Boat Driver: May I ask you, Sir, if it's available in my language?

Jesus: It is. Did you hear that, Gautama? The story...language...the Word again...that which is permanently true. But let me continue.

Another woman was caught in adultery and brought to me. Her accusers wanted to set a trap for me, asserting that the law of Moses said she should be stoned. Strange that the one who committed adultery with her was not there.

Priya: Can I ever identify with that! That's the way our hearts cheat. Then, after we have hurt others, we run.

Jesus: That's it, Priya! The heart is desperately wicked. Who can understand it? This has nothing to do with ignorance. It has everything to do with one's rebellion against God. I change the heart of everyone who comes to me.

There was a third woman. She had lived a life of prostitution. She once came into a room full of self-righteous people, and they were horrified that I would even let her near me, let alone touch me.

You see, that's what legalism does. What do you think would happen to you, Priya, if you hugged that monk or even put your hand on his shoulder?

Priya: Oh my! That would be the end of me…and, for that matter, of him!

Jesus: I told the woman that her pouring the alabaster ointment on me was an expression of worship, and I received it. I *fill* the heart of everyone who comes to me. Her heart was full of the joy of communing with God.

Do you see the sequence, Priya? I disclose; I change; I fill.

Buddha: Before she answers that, isn't that because they were all clearly in need, and they came to you because of their need?

Jesus: There was a teacher by the name of Nicodemus who was a learned man. He came under the cover of darkness to ask how to enter the kingdom of God. I gave him the same answer that I'd given to these others.

You see, Gautama, knowledge and righteousness cannot carry you into the kingdom. You can never truly be righteous until you are redeemed. This is the heart of the difference between you and me. You cannot become righteous by looking deep inside yourself and by meditating.

Priya: So…I cannot bring salvation to myself?

Jesus: No, Priya. Salvation is from above.

The transformation I bring
is not to think oneself
into a different person,
but to yield to the
transcending power of
the Holy Spirit of God.

Buddha talked to you about being reborn in another consciousness and in a different person. The transformation I bring is not to think oneself into a different person, but to yield to the transcending power of the Holy Spirit of God. He works like the wind…you cannot see it, but you can surely see the effects. The person is the same, but the hunger is new, and that new hunger is for the kingdom of God and His righteousness. That's what my work is when one trusts in me as his Lord and Savior. It begins, as I said, with poverty of spirit and leads to purity in heart.

Boat Driver: May I say something here? This conversation is getting uncomfortable. I respect the Buddha. How can he be wrong?

Jesus: Listen to his own words, Wat. He respected the Brahman priests, but he believed they were wrong. One cannot sacrifice truth at the altar of respect. To be sure, truth doesn't eliminate respect. But respect should not be an end in itself. And as you well know, truth is no respecter of persons. That's why I said to the keepers of the Law, "You have heard it said… But *I* say to you…" Respect for the right of another to be wrong does not mean that the wrong is right.

Buddha: The thought is deep…and troublesome. But I have to agree with it.

Priya: May I…may I ask about myself, here? What then happens to all the evil that I lived with in the past, if I cannot do anything about it?

Jesus: I have paid for it, Priya. I have paid for it. Old things can pass away and I can make all things new. I took the evil and suffering of this world. I bore it on my body. I carried your heartaches and your sorrows so that you can remove the weight of wrong and put it on my shoulders. I came into the world to bear those very sins. You may be like a lotus seedling still submerged under the water; someone else may be a full-grown plant. It makes no difference. The Cross is for everyone who thirsts for forgiveness and for eternal life. A child can come to me, as can the most learned. There is only one way.

Buddha: This "suffering that you have borne for my sin…" I almost see it, Jesus. But somehow I don't see how it is just.

Jesus: If justice is what one wants, untempered by mercy, then where is there any recourse for Priya? Justice is fulfilled when one offers to pay the full price of restitution on behalf of another who cannot pay. Karma will never pay, Gautama. Go and ask anyone here if they expect to attain nirvana this time around. They never know if it's paid.

Priya: So you're telling me that as I place my trust in you, I can go back to my room knowing that I've been completely forgiven?

Jesus: I'm telling you more than that. Though this body of yours will die, you will rise again and live forever, because *I* rose from the dead and offer eternal life to everyone who believes in me.

Buddha: Well, I have listened, Jesus. There are superficial similarities to our thoughts but foundational differences. Our messages are worlds apart. The origin and the destiny have no common ground. I tell people that they are born in debt and that they either add to or subtract from that debt by the way they live. *You* tell people to find their inheritance in God.

Jesus: We come to the end of our discussion, Gautama. What would you offer Priya?

Buddha: She knows, I am sure. We call it the Triple Gem. The Buddha—enlightenment; the Dhamma—the teaching; and the Sangha—the community.

Jesus: Look at them one at a time, Gautama.

First, the Buddha. According to your teaching, you personally no longer exist, nor will she. Nonexistence is the first gem.

The Dhamma. The teaching has no eternal Word to preserve, no absolute to be guided by. That's the second gem.

The Sangha. The community consists of those who believe no self exists and move toward not desiring anything, including the friendship of others. That's the third gem.

You know, Gautama, one day a man looking for precious pearls came upon a pearl of great price. He traded everything he had to obtain this pearl.

I am that Pearl of great price. Through me, Priya can bring the rule of God into her heart. That's what I mean when I say that the kingdom of God is within a person and not imposed by any rule from without. I will give her the purity that she thinks she can never recover. I will bring her into the presence of God.

Priya: My choice, then, is the Triple Gem or the Pearl of great price?

Jesus: Your choice is either to obliterate your self or to find your self. Desolation or communion. Let me tell you, finally, what this communion with God means. But first, let's get back to the boat.

Priya: Jesus, when we get back to the boat, could you please get me my medicine from the brown bottle in my bag? It's to help with the pain...I'm afraid it does nothing for the disease.

Jesus: That's the way it is with man's attempt to gain favor with God, too. All that you've seen here—the ceremony, the superstition—is dealing with the pain. It doesn't get at the disease.

Where's your cup, Priya?

Priya: I put it back in the bag so nobody would come in contact with it.

Respect for the right
of another to be wrong
does not mean that the
wrong is right.

Jesus: Fill it with water for me, please.

Priya: What're you doing? Wait! No, don't! Why...why did you drink from my cup? My germs are all over that cup! Why did you do this to yourself?

Jesus: I did it for you, Priya, in even greater measure than this. No one wants to drink from your cup. Buddha said that you filled your cup with your choices and so you alone must drink it. I say to you something different.

Read my Word, Priya. Shortly before those who wanted me crucified came to take me, I was alone in prayer, in communion with my heavenly Father. As I prayed, I knew that the cup of suffering and death that I was to drink from was for all mankind. I knew it was a bitter cup. It contained the sins and the shame of the whole world. In agreeing to drink from that cup I knew it would even separate me for a moment from my Father. That desolation was the most fearsome thing I was called upon to do. But in drinking from that cup, I was able to offer the gift of eternal life to all who would accept it.

Priya: You mean you've taken a drink from the cup of all human suffering and sin...and even death?

Jesus: Yes, I have.

A thousand years before that moment, one of the psalmists of Israel spoke of it. Out of the depths of pain he cried:

The LORD is gracious and righteous;
our God is full of compassion.
I believed; therefore I said,
"I am greatly afflicted."
And in my dismay I said,
"All men are liars."
How can I repay the LORD
for all his goodness to me?
I will lift up the cup of salvation
and call on the name of the LORD.

I offer my cup for yours, Priya. At the Cross I drank your cup. Now I give you a fresh cup of eternal life. You can drink from it.

This is your chance, Priya. Take it freely.

Buddha: It's getting a bit dark; it's time to return. Who'll pay the boatman? I don't keep any money with me.

Boat Driver: No need for it. What I've learned has been of infinite worth.

Jesus: But then you have to bear the cost.

Boat Driver: Please consider it my gift.

Jesus: Before you leave, Wat, may I offer you my gift too?

With just a slight change of intonation, your name would mean "temple," wouldn't it?

The Cross is for everyone
who thirsts for forgiveness
and for eternal life.

Boat Driver: Yes, but I could never make that change because only a building can be a temple.

Jesus: I have said in my Word that each person is meant to be a temple, and I make my home in each one who invites me to come in. I offer you that relationship as well.

Boat Driver: I'll never forget you, Sir!

Priya: I suppose neither of you can go back to my home with me?

Buddha: No, I can't.

Jesus: I can.

Epilogue

As the boatman drops me off, I am keenly aware that just he and I have been on this trip. The presence of three others in conversation was an imaginary scenario.

But it is not imaginary that both Buddha and Jesus have left their words with us. Buddhism is a well-thought-through belief that is bereft of God. More accurately, it's a philosophy of how one can be good without God, pulling oneself up by one's own moral bootstraps. Its allurement is obvious. In a very subtle way it is the ultimate crowning of the individual with total autonomy, while at the same time it declares that the self is an illusion.

It argues for impermanence with the force of a permanent injunction.

It encourages thought and contemplation, but the final destination is thoughtlessness and oblivion.

It is a religion without God, without a final word, and without even a final existence.

Why has it gained such a following? For the very reason that Adam and Eve broke their fellowship with God: They wanted to be independent of Him and to define their own reality even though God had told them that in the day they broke His command, they would surely die. In a similar manner, Buddha claimed to be more enlightened than God, and death was his inevitable end.

But there's a more subtle attraction to Buddhism—the sense of being in control and fully insulated from the world of care. If you break off all attachments, you cease to worry. If you have no loves, you will never have a broken heart. If you cease to love, you cease to suffer. If you do not desire, you can never lose. That is it in a nutshell.

Suppose you were waiting to check in for a flight to a particular destination and had your suitcase beside you. If you were to step away for a few minutes, leaving your luggage unguarded, what recourse would you have should that bag be stolen? You certainly couldn't go to the airline counter and demand it back, because it was in your care when you lost it. You were in control, no one else. But if it was lost after you had already checked it in, it's the responsibility of the airline to find it for you. You had committed it to their care.

In Buddhism, everything is in your care. All losses are yours. There is no "other" to whom you can go. But the message of Jesus Christ is a very different story. The apostle Paul came to realize how hollow his impeccable credentials were, though he had once boasted of them as his claim to perfection. There came a moment of surrender when he laid them all at the feet of Jesus and said, "I know whom I have believed, and am convinced that he is able to guard what I have entrusted to him for that day" (2 Timothy 1:12).

Turn all your loves, your attachments, your affections over to Jesus Christ, and He guards for you what He wants to bless you with. By delivering into His keeping all that is important to you, you will find that He preserves for you the beauty of your loves and protects you from the illusion of autonomy.

Jesus Christ came to give us a life of fullness, not detachment, a life that will be eternal, not impermanent. His name is Jesus, the Scriptures say, because He saves us from our sins. His name is also Emmanuel—God with us. He is called Wonderful Counselor, Almighty God, Everlasting Father, the Prince of Peace.

Priya died feeling orphaned by this world—she needed a Father.

She died overwhelmed with questions—He is the Wonderful Counselor.

She died distraught—He is the Prince of Peace.

She died alone—He is Emmanuel, God with us.

He promised never to leave us or forsake us. Jesus is who Priya needed.

In that sense, He was very much in that boat and is not far from any of us. That each one of us can know Him is not a stretch of the imagination.

More from Ravi Zacharias and the Great Conversations Series!

Have you ever wondered what Jesus would say to Hitler? Or to Buddha? Maybe you have a friend who practices another religion or admires a more contemporary figure. Drop in on a conversation between Jesus and these well-known individuals whose search for the meaning of life took them in many directions—and influenced millions. Popular scholar Ravi Zacharias sets a captivating scene by developing an imaginary dialogue between Christ and each historical figure as God's true nature is explored and Jesus' warm impassioned concern for all people is revealed.